GODS & GODDESSES
FANTASY ART ADULT COLORING BOOK

Copyright © 2020 Vivid Publishers
Illustrated by Chinthaka Herath
Design & layout by Intense Media

All rights reserved. No part of this publication may be reproduced, distributed or transmitted in any form or by any means including photocopying, recording or other electronic or mechanical methods, without the prior written permission of the Publisher/ Chinthaka Herath.

ISBN-13: 9798650722267

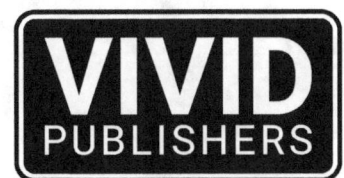

INTRODUCTION

Thank you for purchasing 'Gods & Goddesses', a fantasy art adult coloring book by Chinthaka Herath. This book features 24 pages of enchanting characters from Greek Mythology.

Open up this book to color away your stress and enter a fantasy world of Gods & Goddesses along with their counterparts & animal companions.

All the illustrations are hand drawn by the artist.

You can use any coloring medium from pencils to markers as long as they have a fine tip.

A note on the use of markers: Even though the illustrations are printed one per page, to give additional protection please place a thick paper or cardboard beneath the page you are coloring so that the ink will not bleed through to the next page.

Subscribe at our website to get a FREE 10 Page PDF Sampler 'Fantasy Art Adult Coloring Collection' featuring pages from our three adult coloring books August Reverie 1, 2 and Saga: Fire & Water! Plus, news on discounts, free pages, contests and more!

 www.vividpublishers.com

We would love to see your completed art. You can reach us at:

 fb.com/VividPublishers

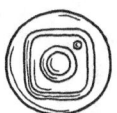 @VividPublishers

Also, we welcome you to join our Facebook group to share your art, see other colorists' art, enter exciting contests plus more!

 fb.com/groups/VividPublishers

Thank you for your continued support and interest in our adult coloring books. We hope you enjoy coloring the pages as much as we did creating them. Happy Coloring!

CONTENTS

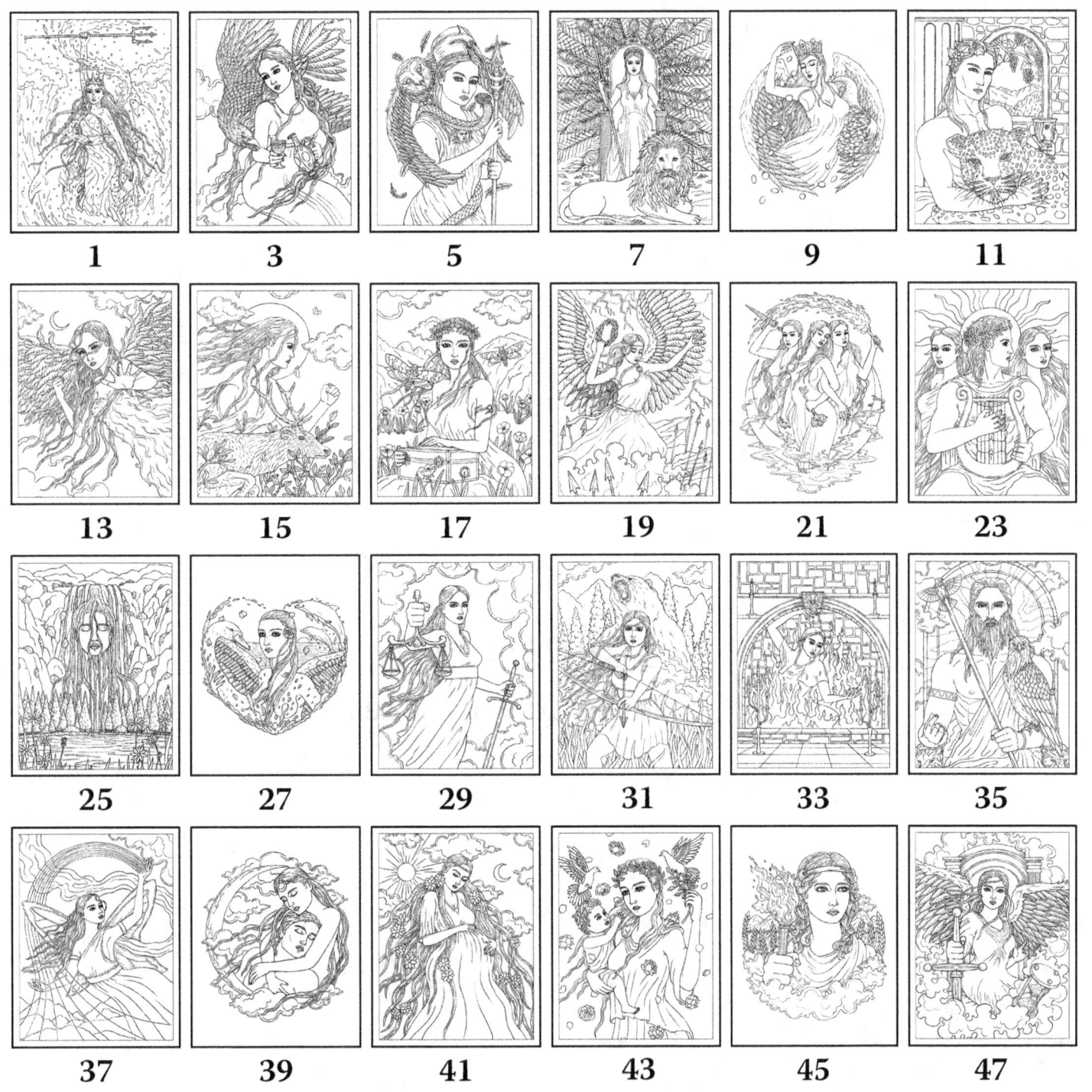

1) AMPHITRITE   3) HEBE   5) ATHENA   7) HERA
9) TYCHE   11) DIONYSUS   13) NYX   15) ARTEMIS
17) PANDORA   19) NIKE   21) HEKATE   23) APOLLO
25) GAEA   27) APHRODITE   29) THEMIS   31) ATALANTA
33) HESTIA   35) ZEUS   37) IRIS   39) SELENE
41) LETO   43) EIRENE   45) DEMETER   47) NEMESIS

AMPHITRITE

Queen goddess of the sea.

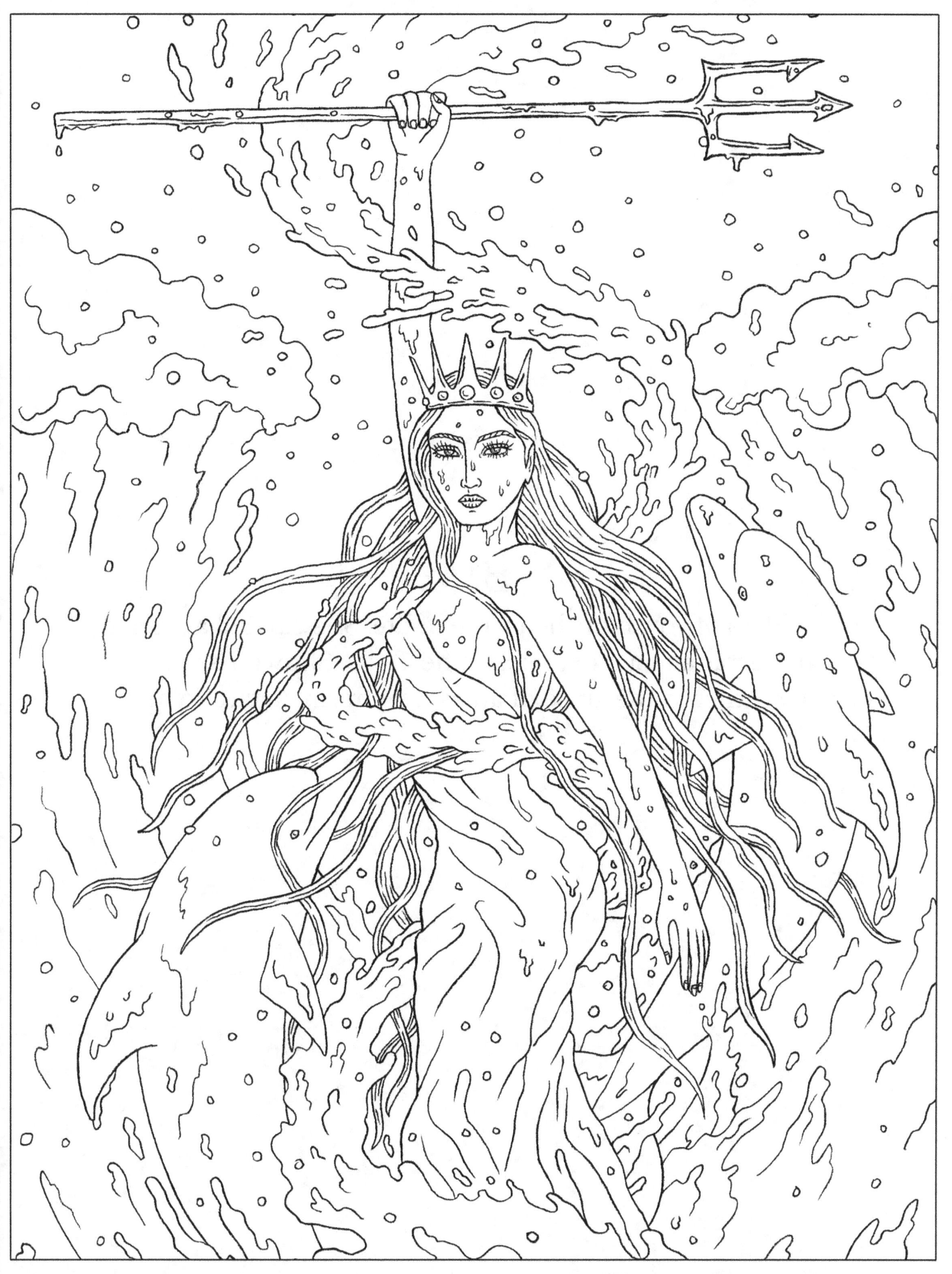

Hebe

Goddess of youth or the prime of life. She carried a pitcher of nectar and a cup to serve the Gods. Shown here with her father in the guise of an eagle, offering a cup to him.

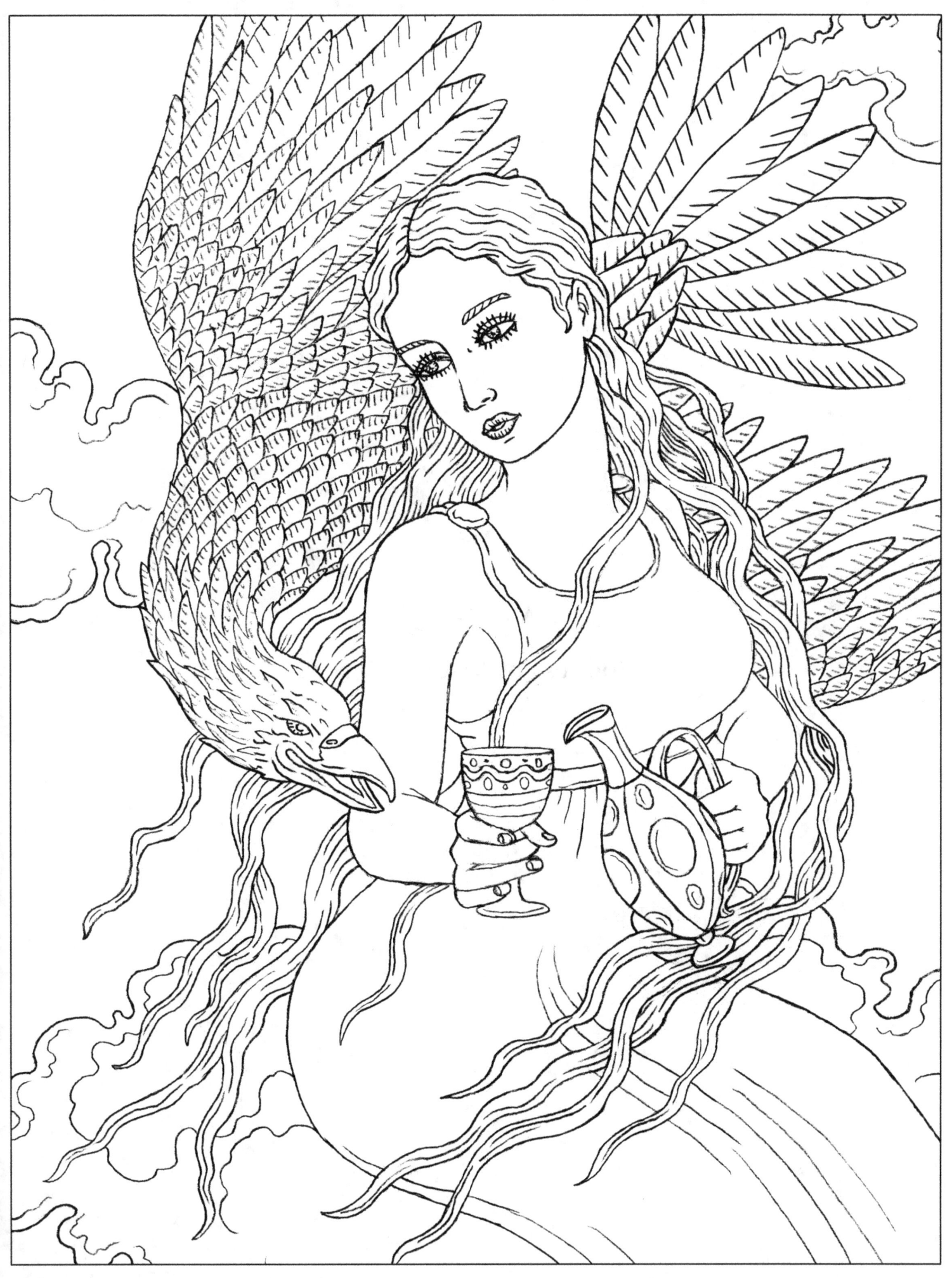

Athena

Goddess of wisdom & war.

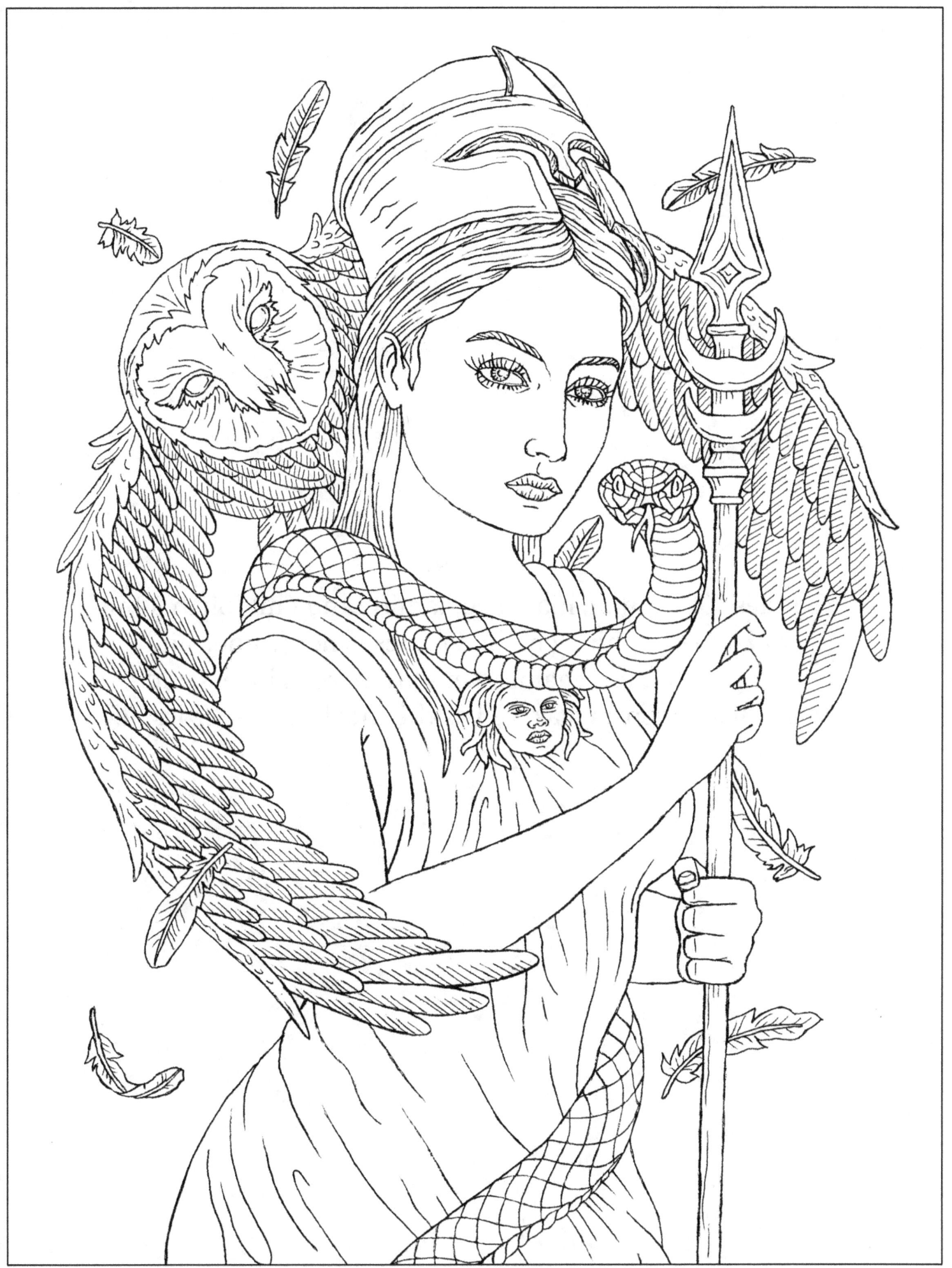

Hera

Goddess of women, marriage, family, and childbirth. One of Hera's defining characteristics is her jealous and vengeful nature against Zeus' numerous lovers and illegitimate offspring, as well as the mortals who cross her.

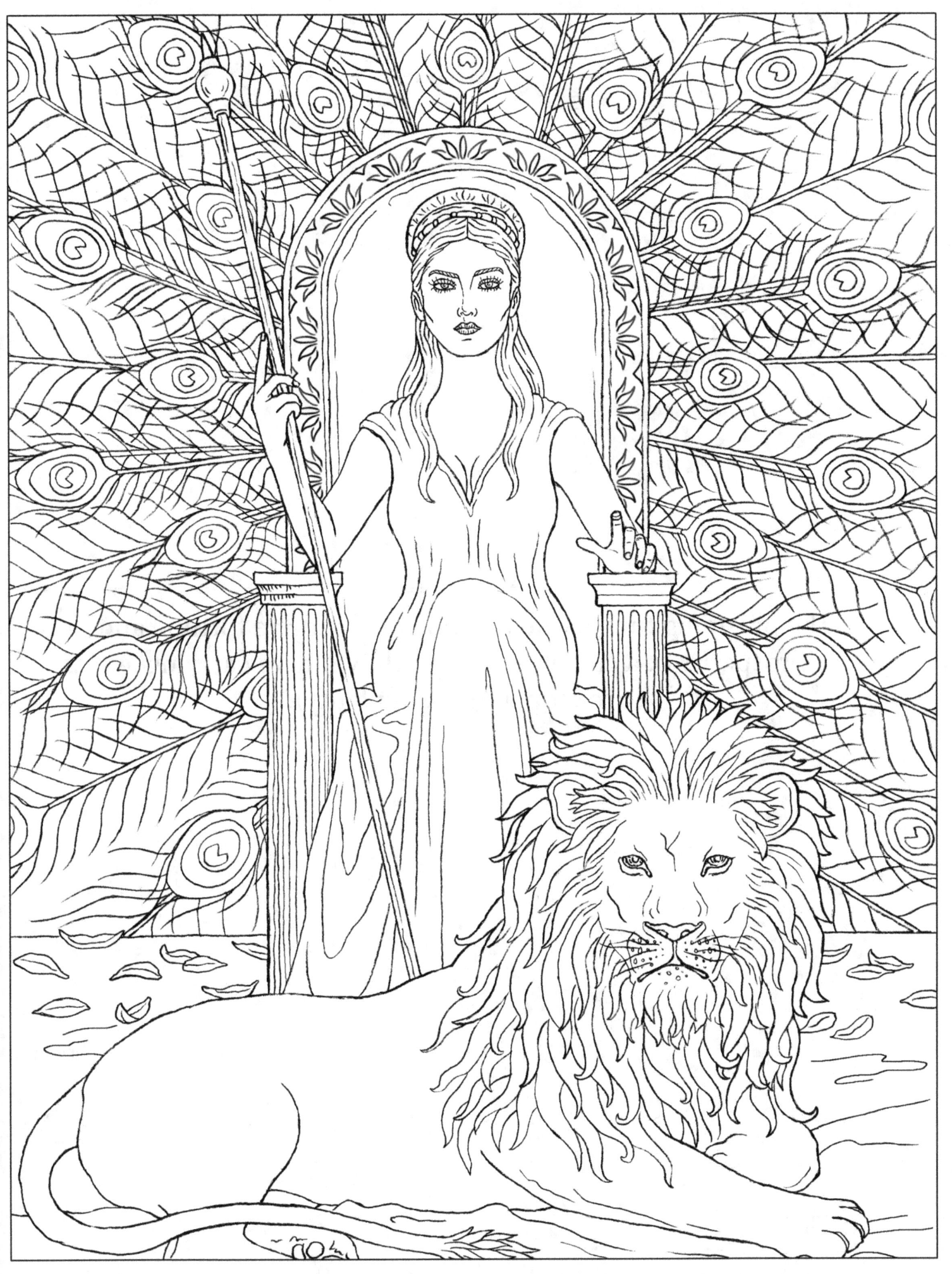

Tyche

The presiding tutelary deity who governed the fortune and prosperity of a city, its destiny. Shown here carrying a cornucopia (horn of plenty).

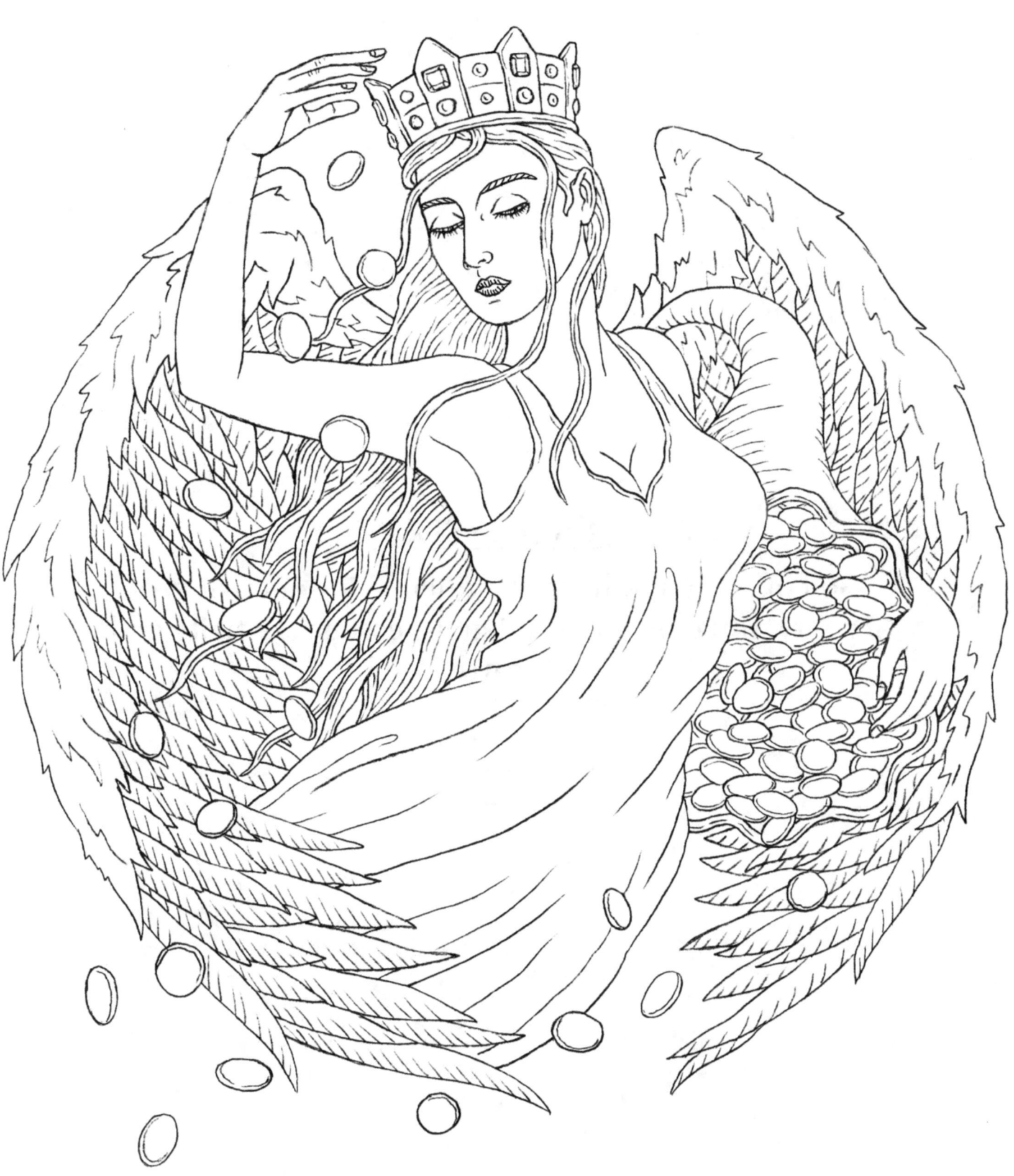

Dionysus

God of the grape-harvest, winemaking and wine, of fertility, ritual madness, religious ecstasy, festivity and theatre.

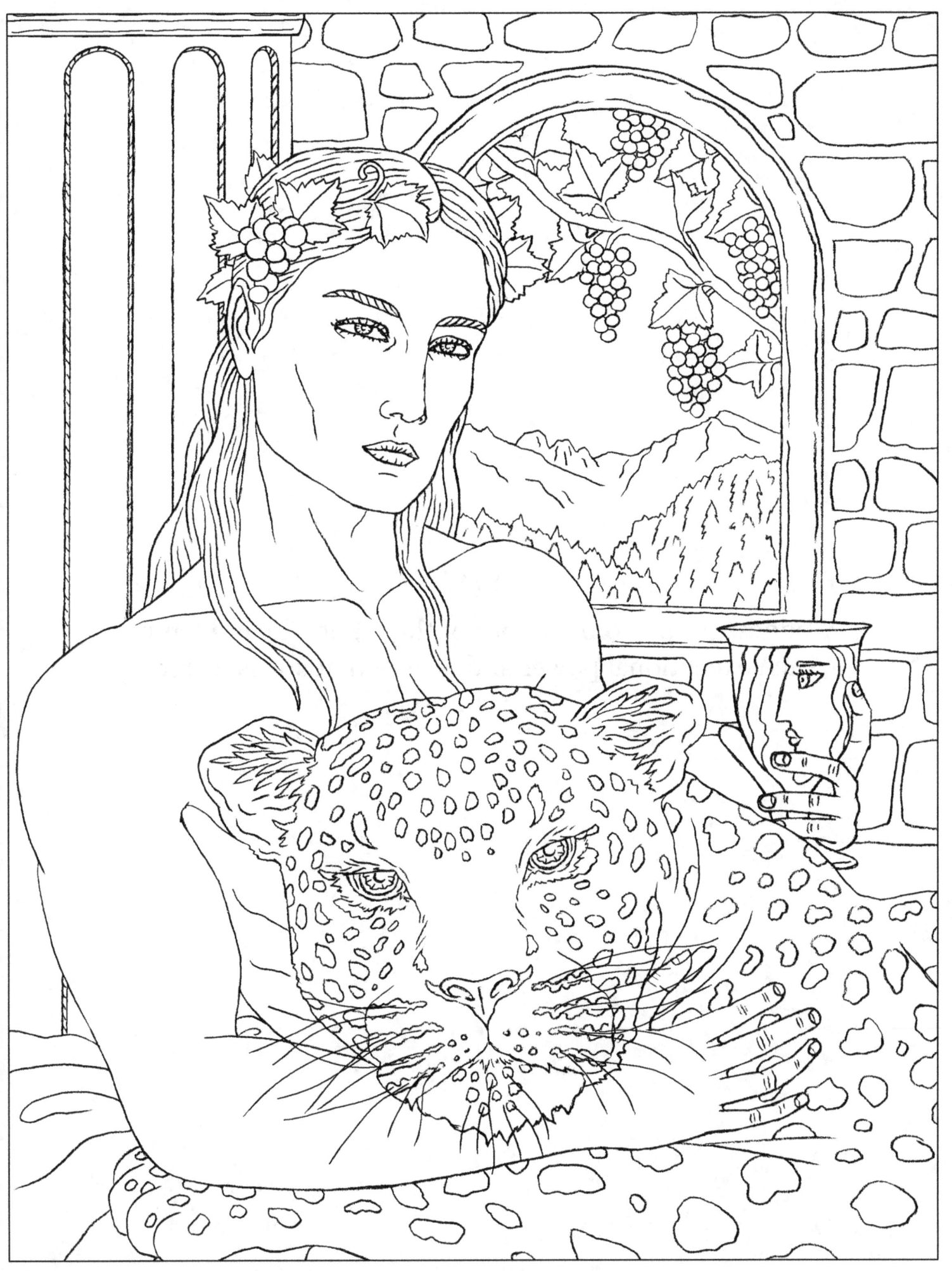

Nyx

Goddess (or personification) of the night. She is a figure of such exceptional power and beauty that she is feared by Zeus himself.

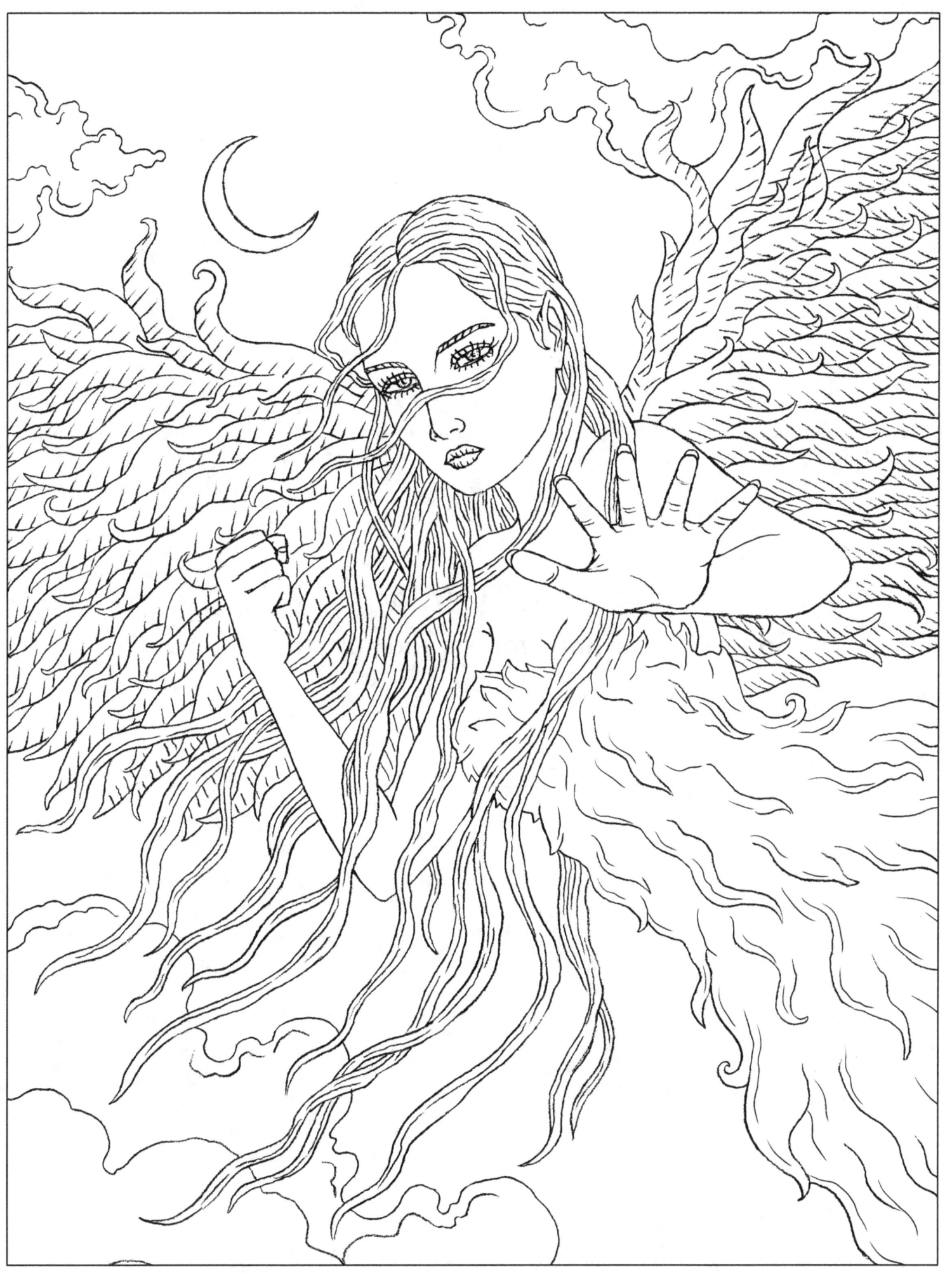

Artemis

Goddess of the hunt, forests and hills, the Moon and archery.

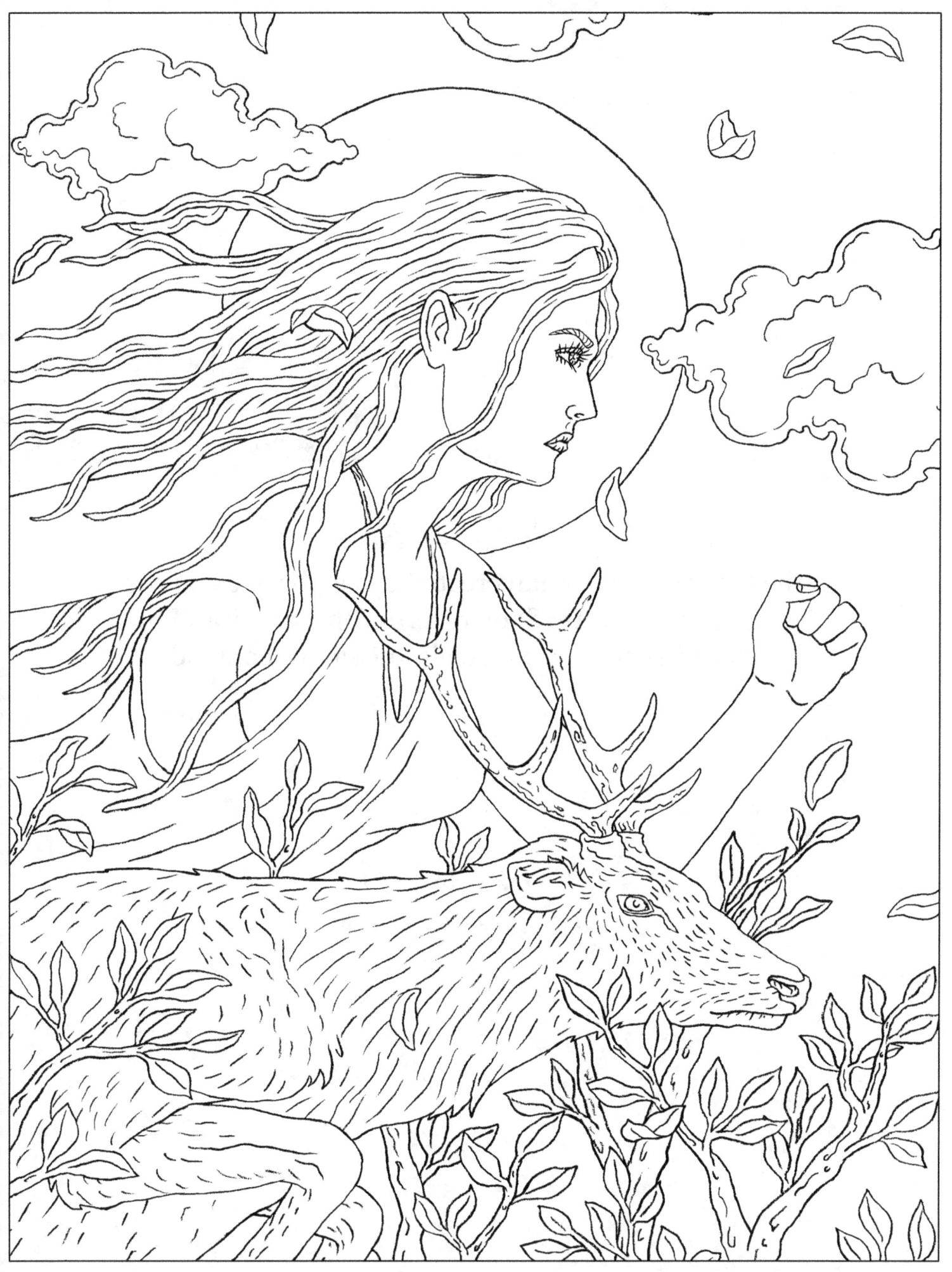

Pandora

The first human woman created by Hephaestus on the instructions of Zeus. Shown here with 'Pandora's Box', just before releasing all evils known to mankind.

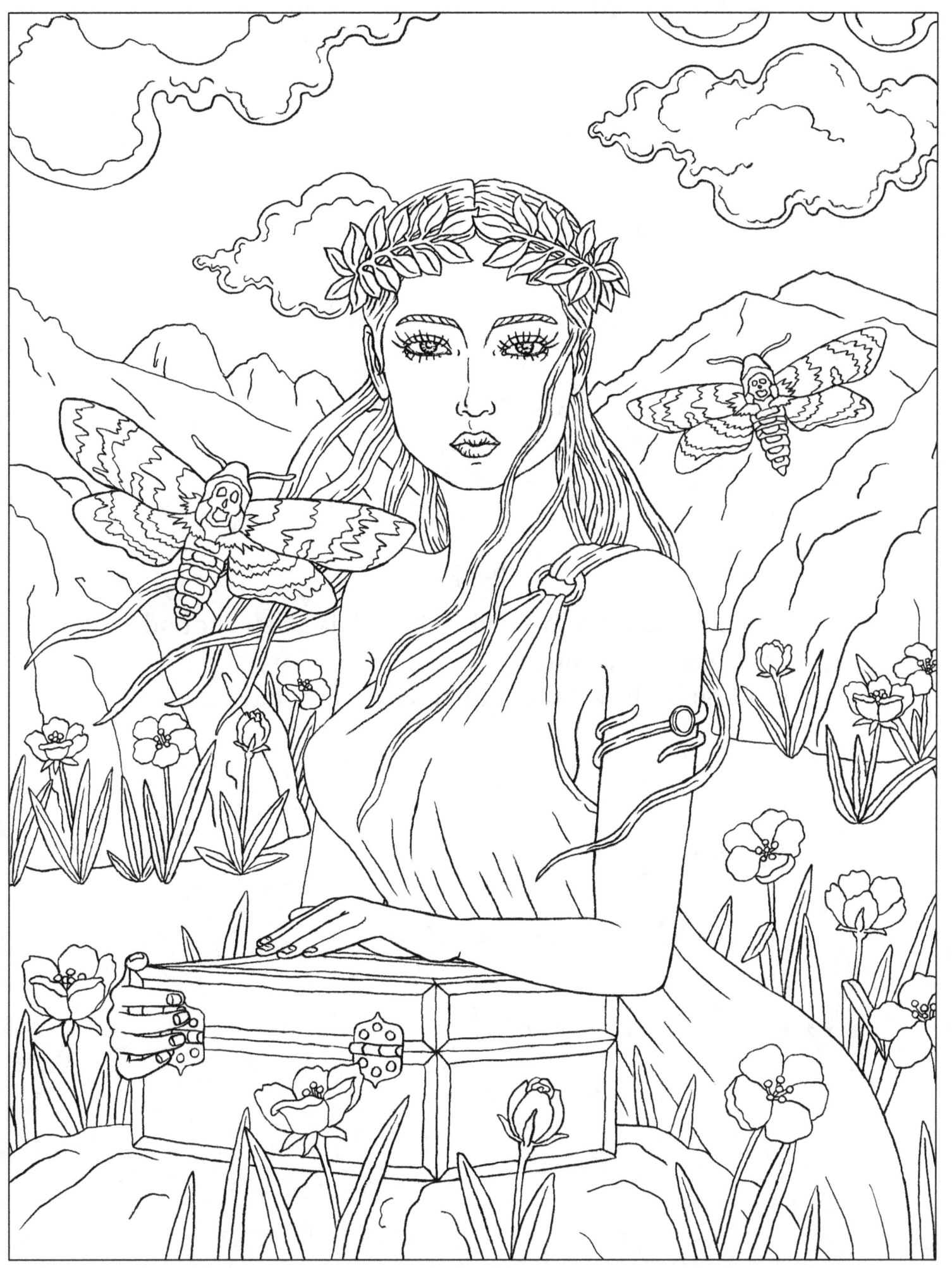

Nike

Goddess who personified victory. Nike flew around battlefields rewarding the victors with glory and fame, symbolized by a wreath of laurel leaves (bay leaves).

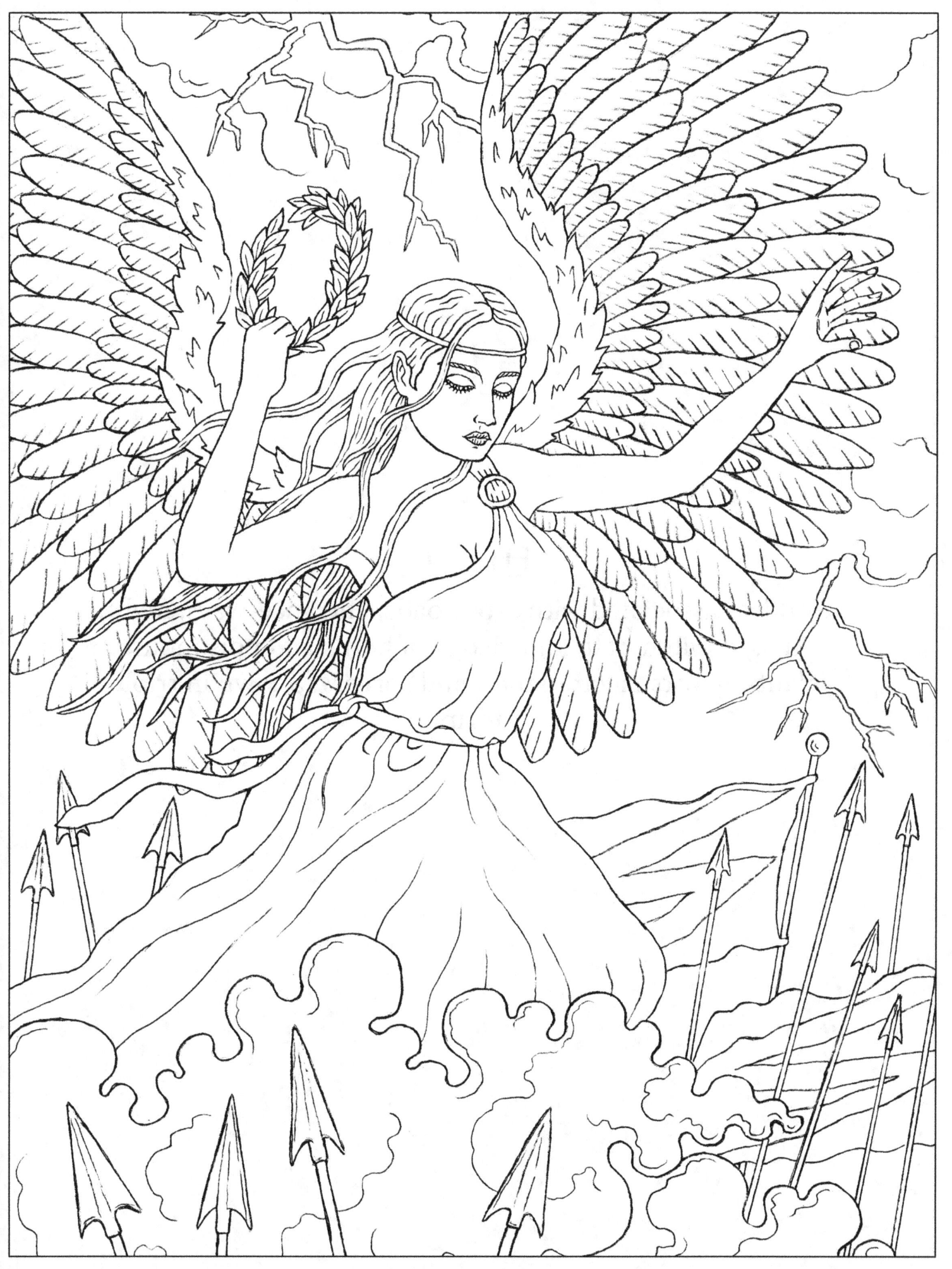

Hekate

Goddess associated with crossroads, entrance-ways, night, magic, witchcraft, knowledge of herbs and poisonous plants, ghosts, necromancy, and sorcery. Shown in triple form.

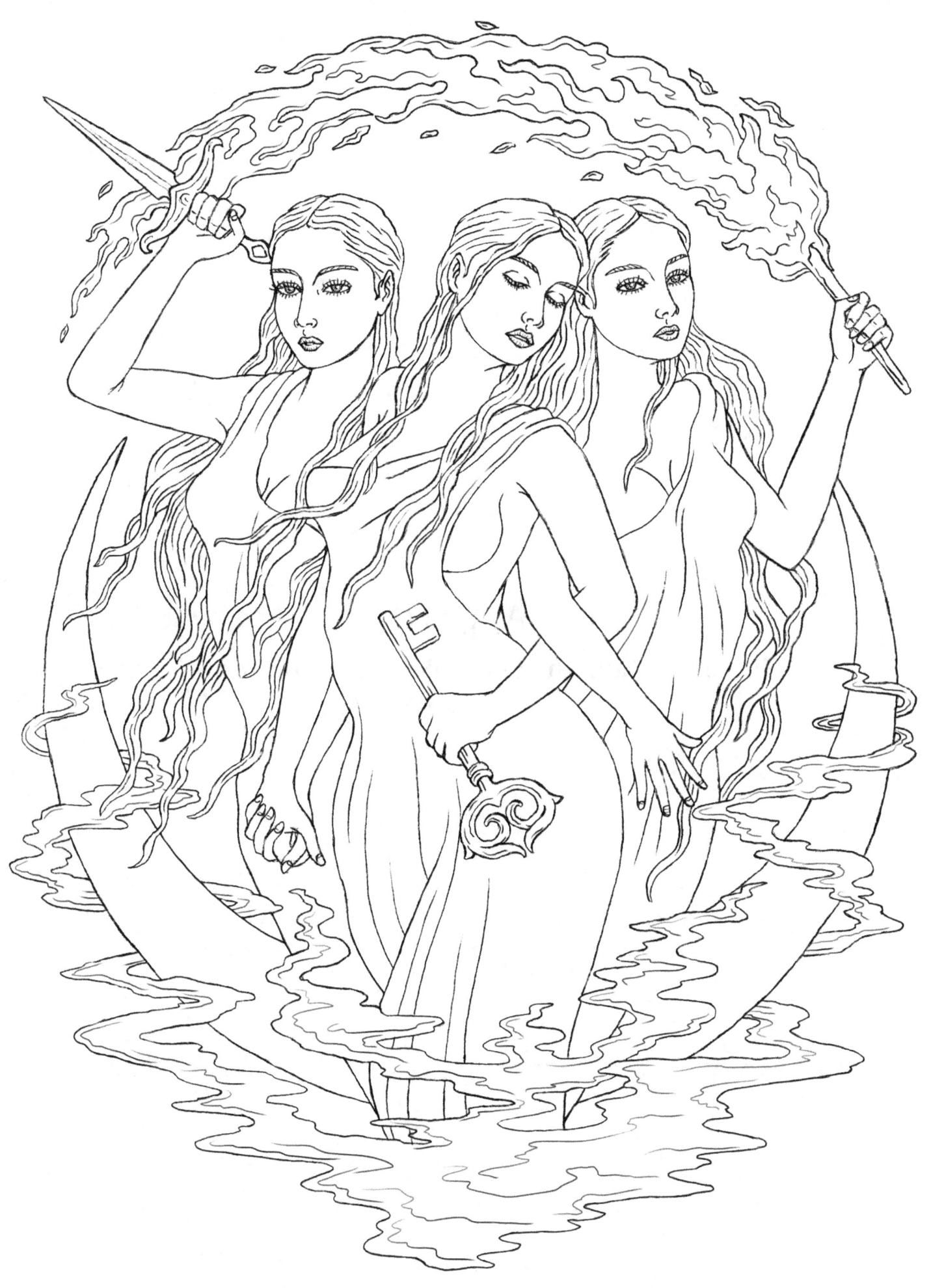

Apollo

God of the Sun, the light, the music and prophecy.

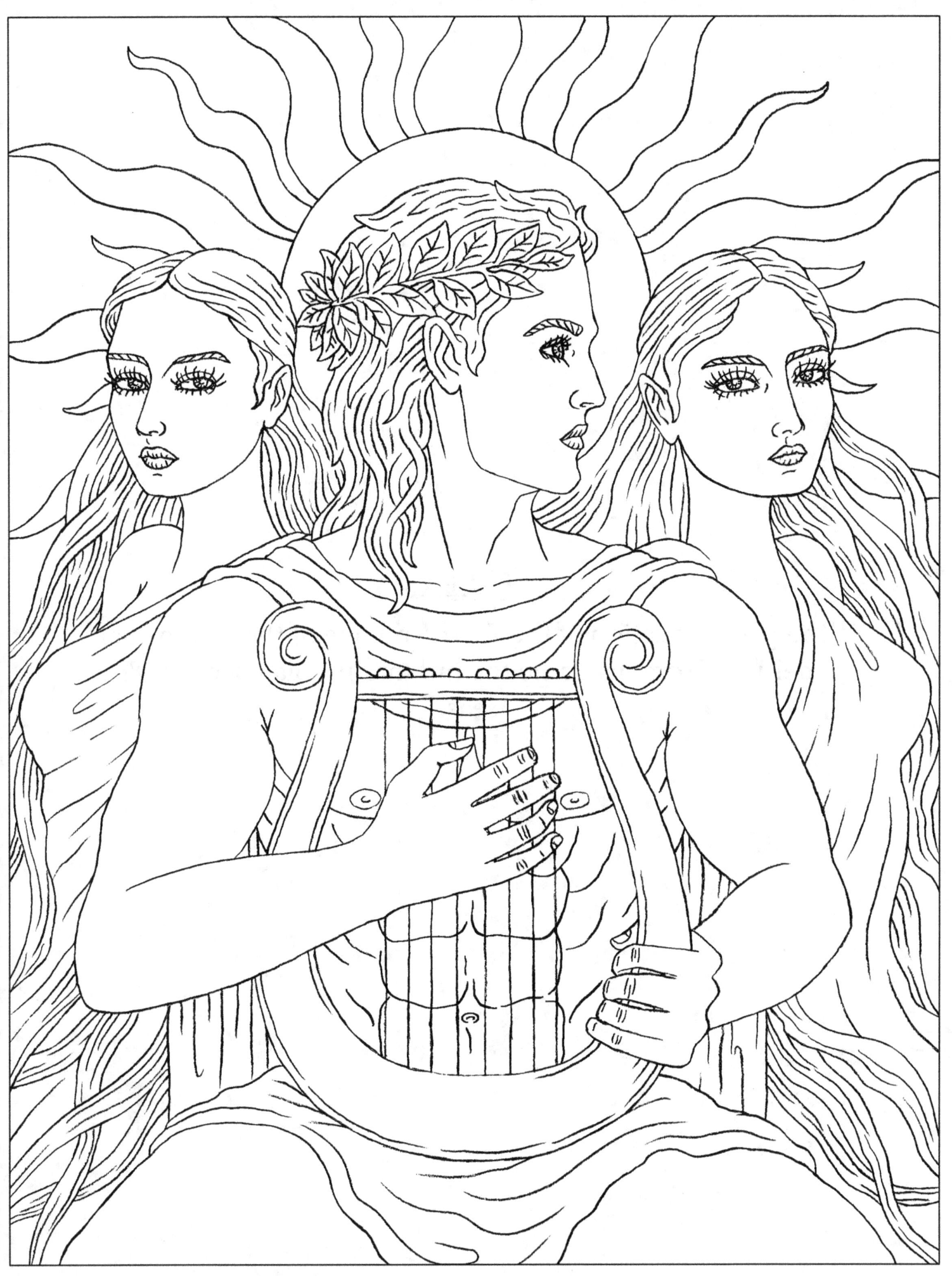

Gaea

The personification of the Earth and one of the primordial deities. From her came the mountains, plains, rivers & seas.

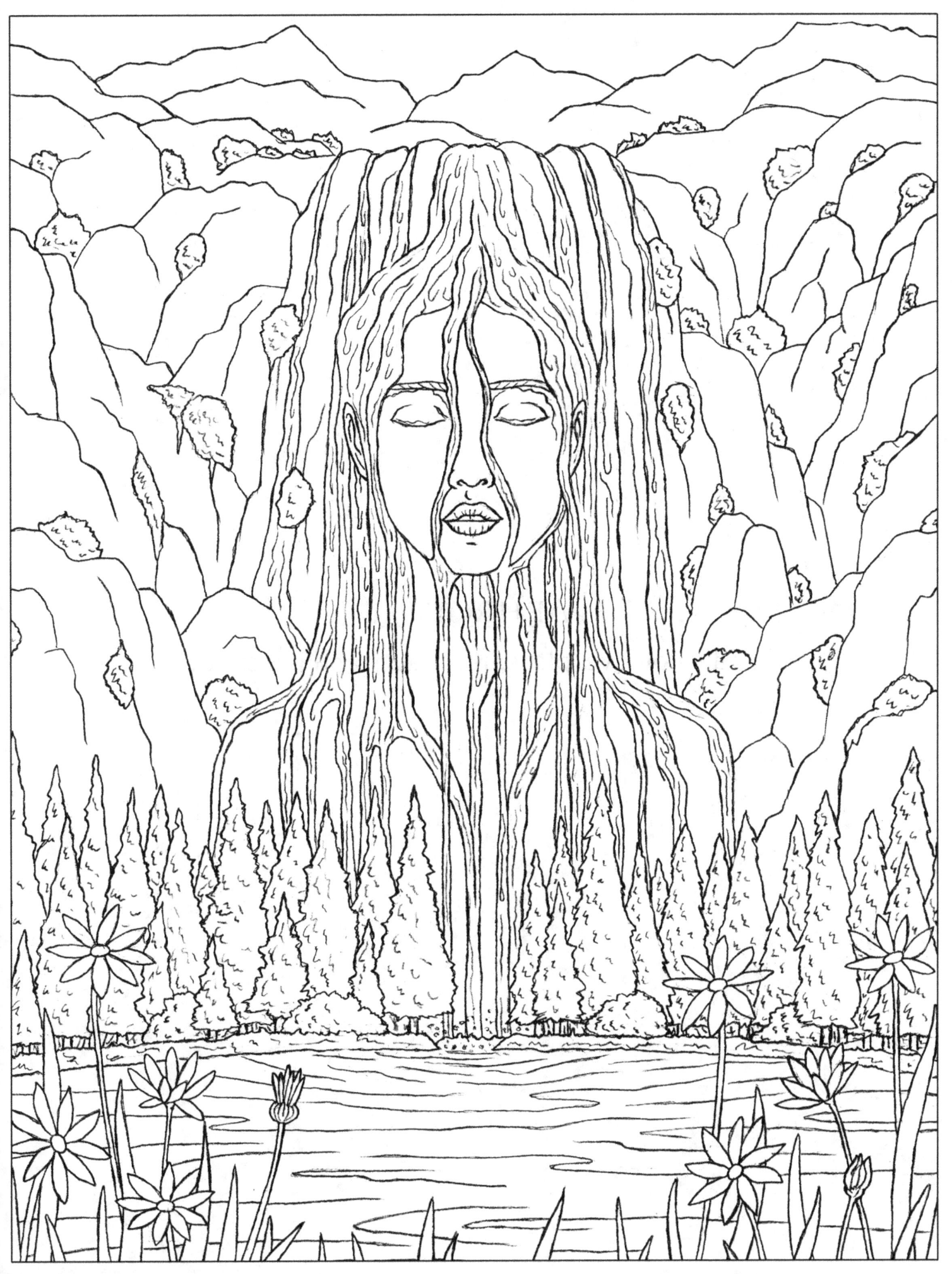

Aphrodite
Goddess of love, pleasure, beauty and procreation.

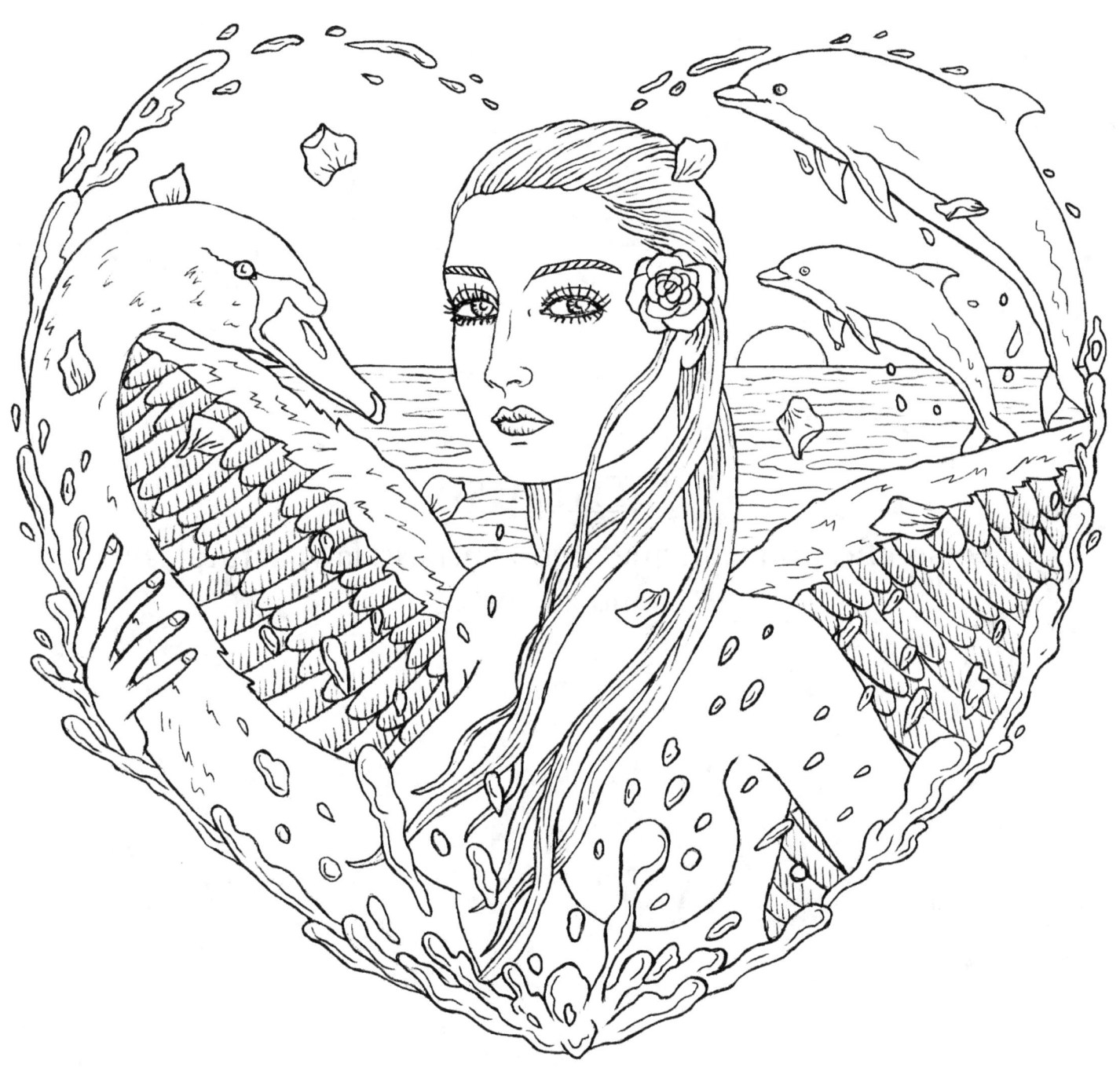

Themis

Personification of divine order, fairness, law, natural law, and custom.

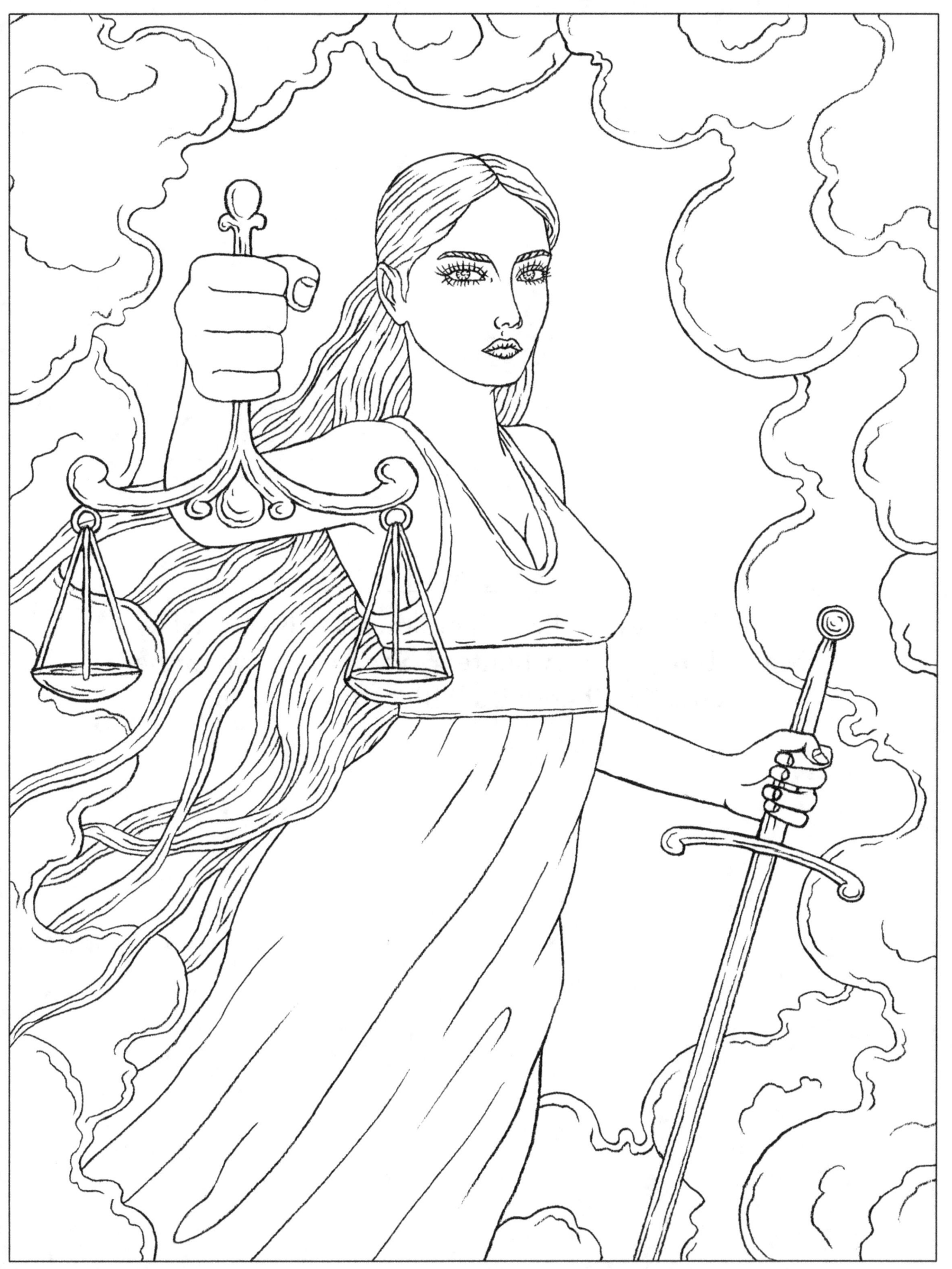

ATALANTA

Left in the forest to die by her father, she was saved by a bear & brought up by hunters. She was known for her athletic & hunting abilities equal to men.

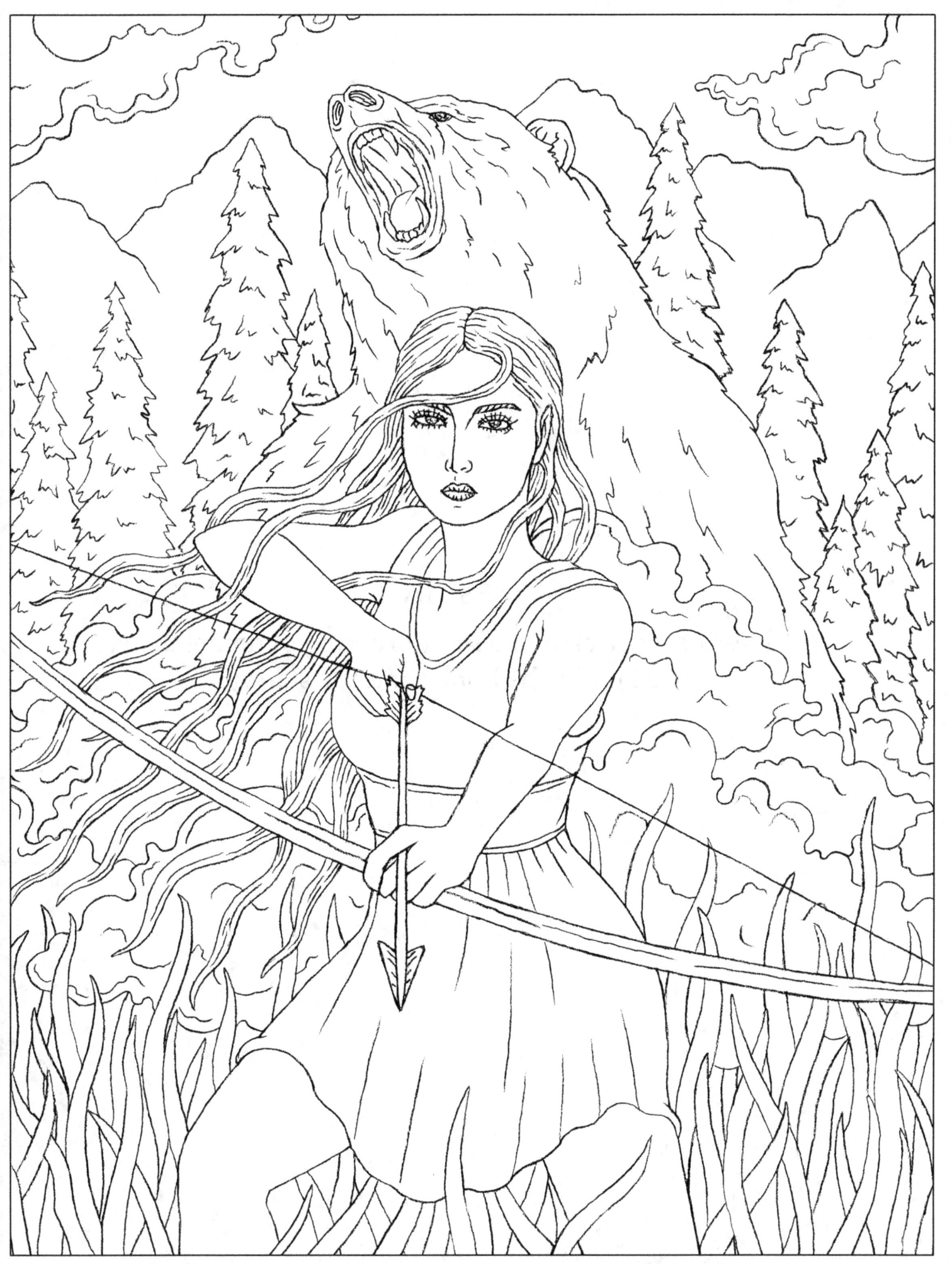

Hestia

Goddess of the hearth, the right ordering of domesticity, the family, the home, and the state.

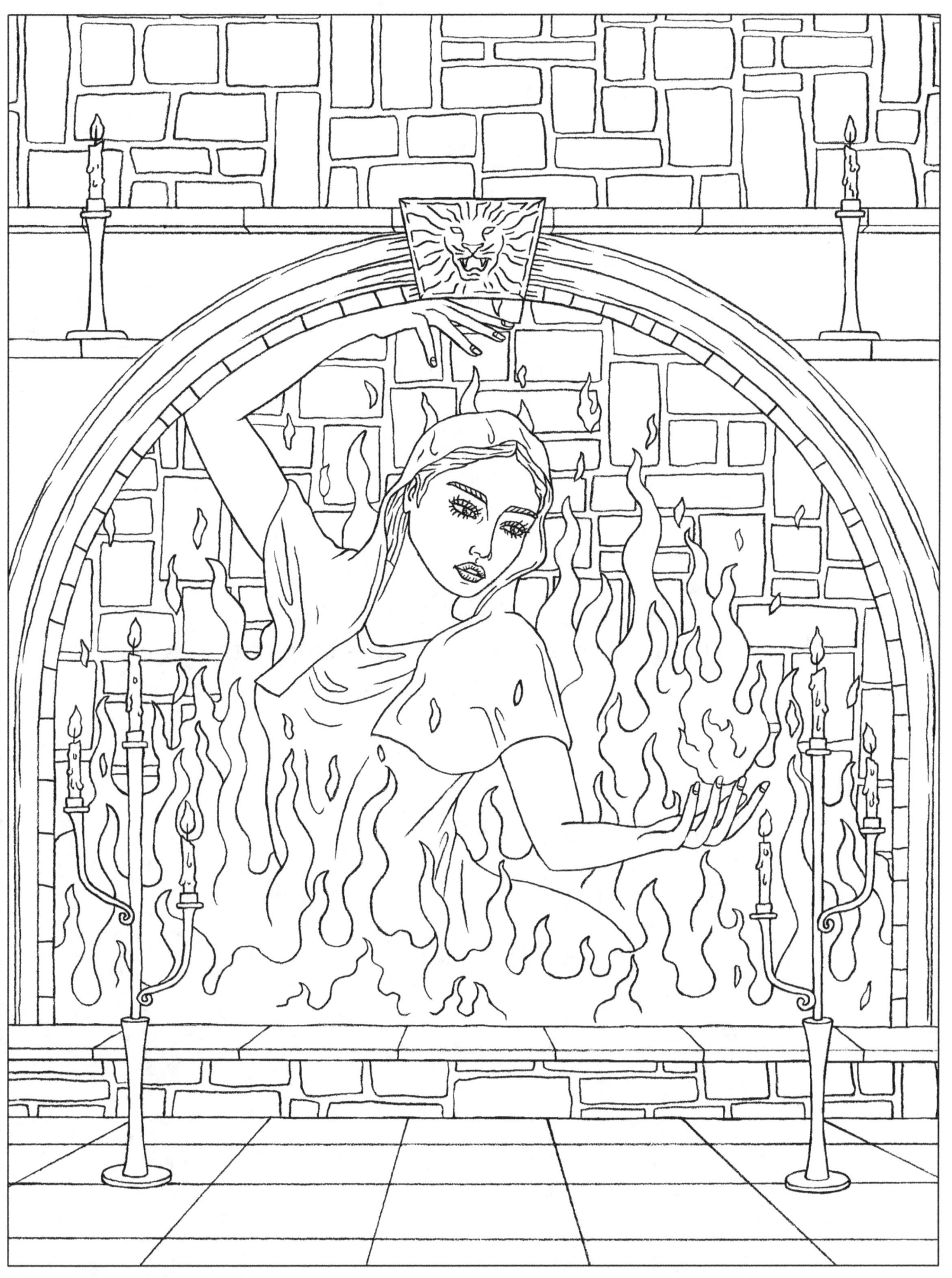

Zeus

The sky and thunder god, who rules as king of the gods of Mount Olympus.

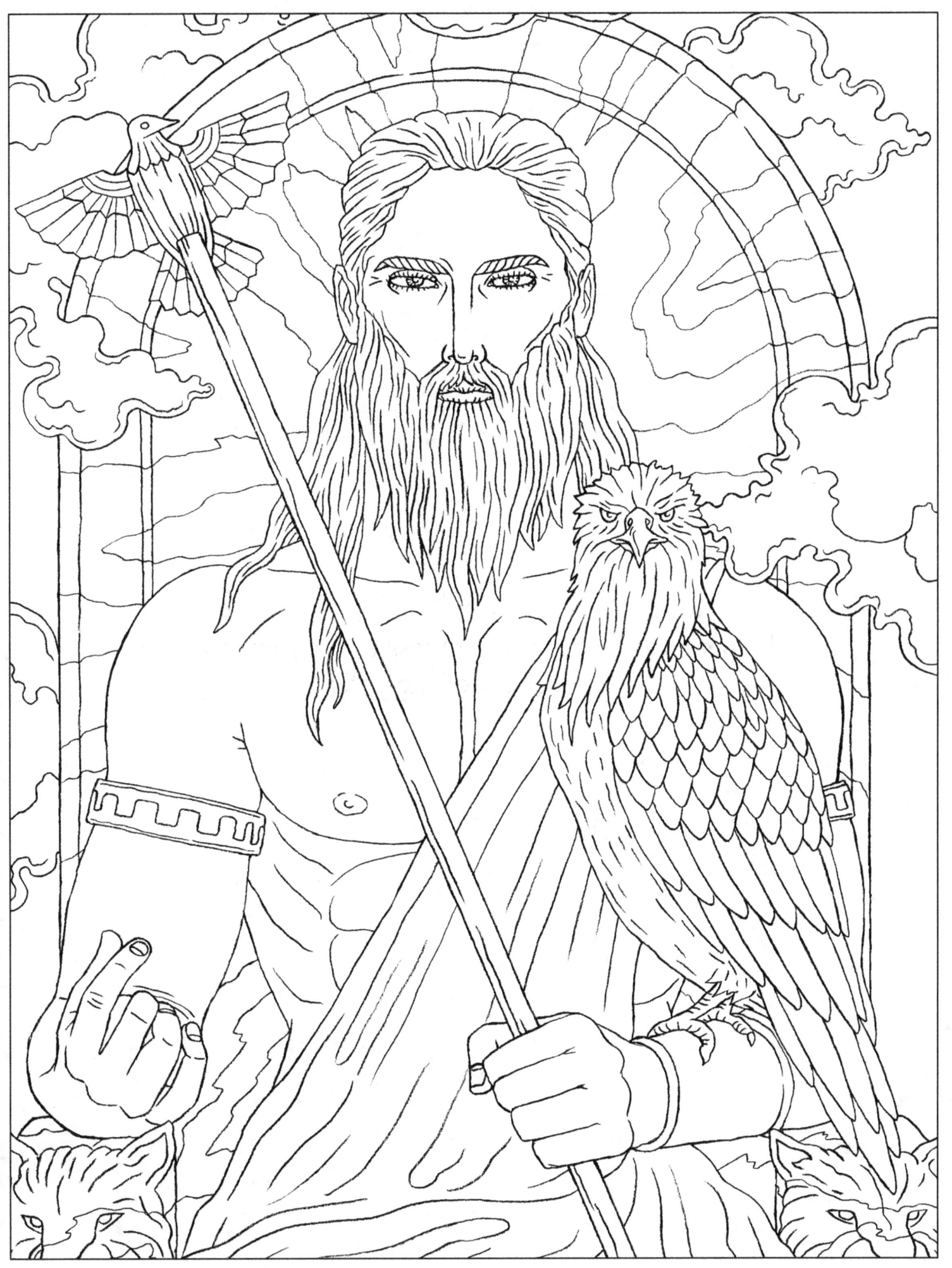

Iris

The personification and goddess of the rainbow and messenger of the gods.

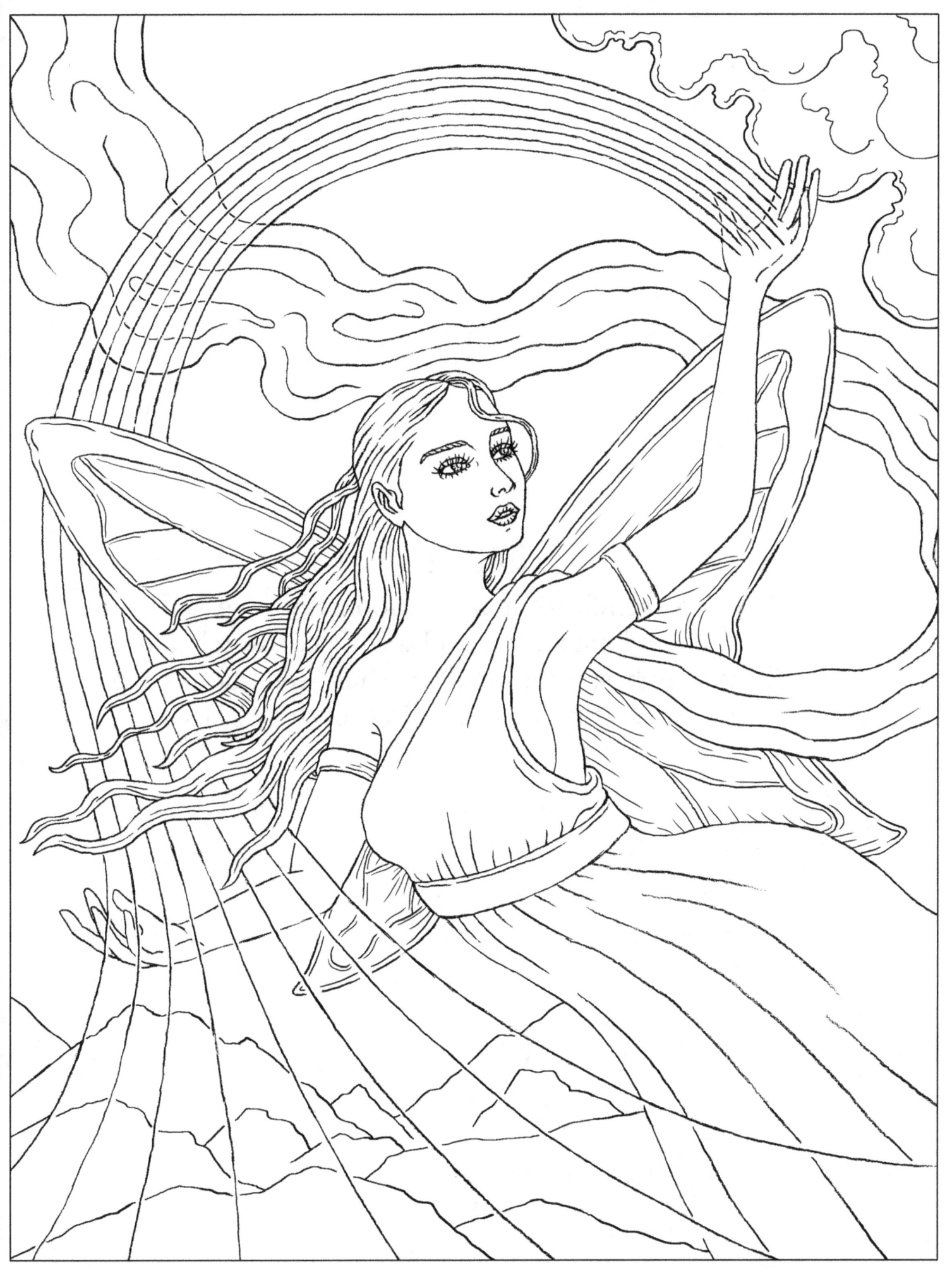

Selene

Goddess & personification of the Moon. She loves a mortal man named Endymion. It is said that Selene watched him while he slept beside his cattle. He has been put to sleep forever in return of everlasting youth by Zeus.

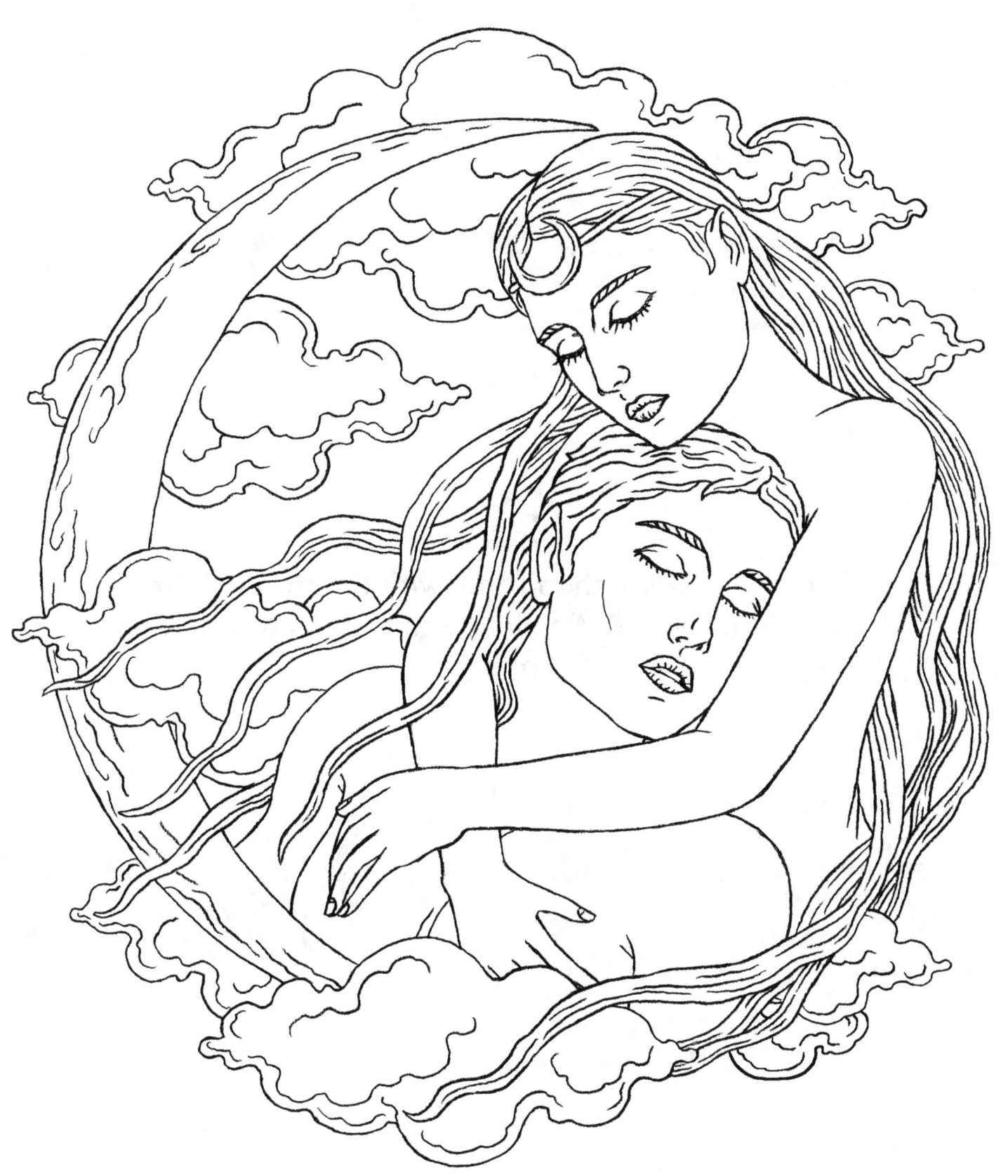

Leto

Goddess of motherhood and, with her twin children Artemis (Moon) & Apollo (Sun), a protectress of the young.

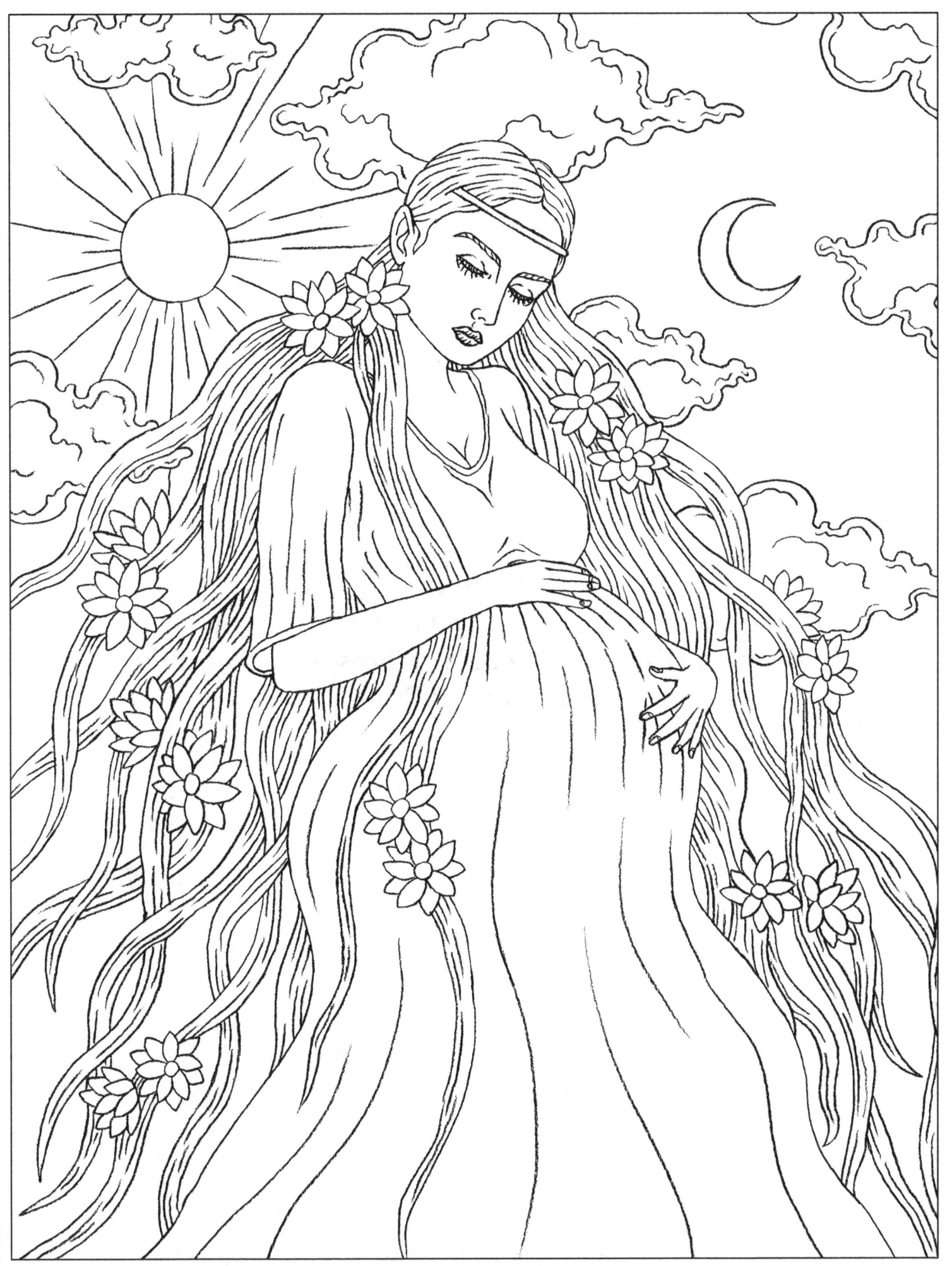

Eirene

The personification of Peace. Shown here carrying Plutus (Plenty), as an allegory of Plenty prospering under the protection of Peace.

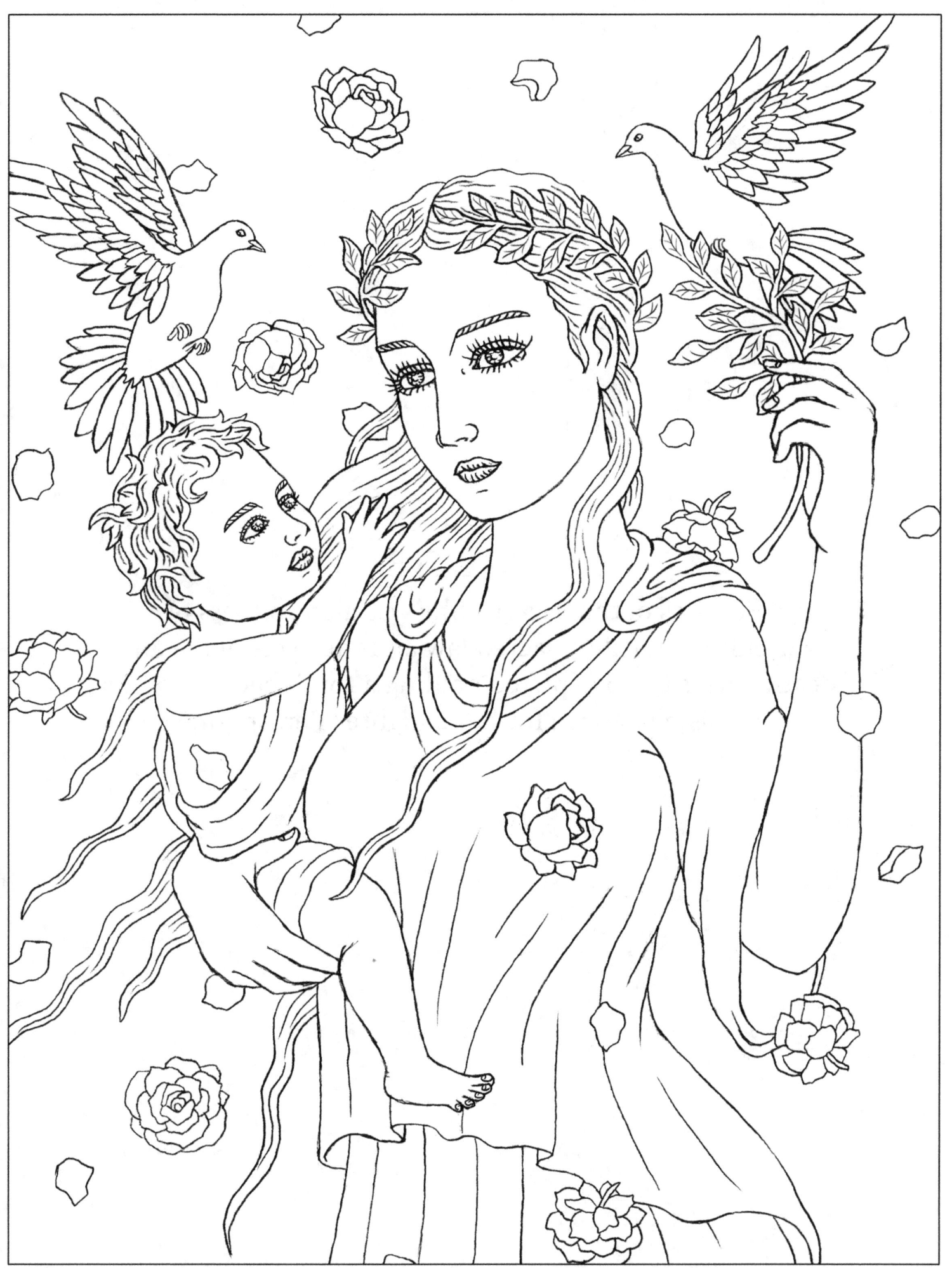

Demeter

Goddess of the harvest. She was also goddess of agriculture, fertility, sacred law and the cycle of life and death. She is often depicted holding a torch because of her persistent search for her daughter Persephone.

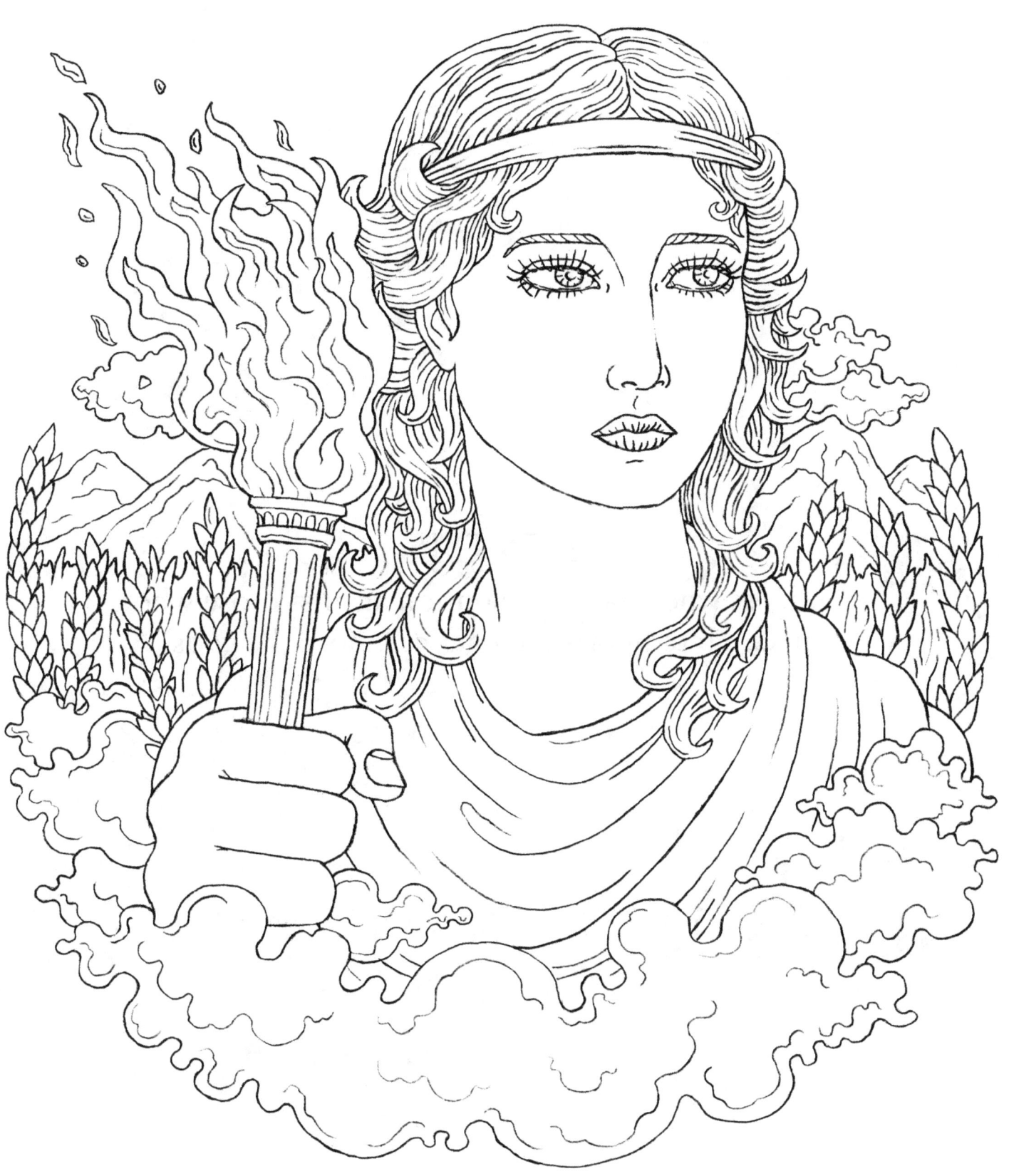

Nemesis
Goddess who enacts retribution against those who succumb to hubris (arrogance before the gods)

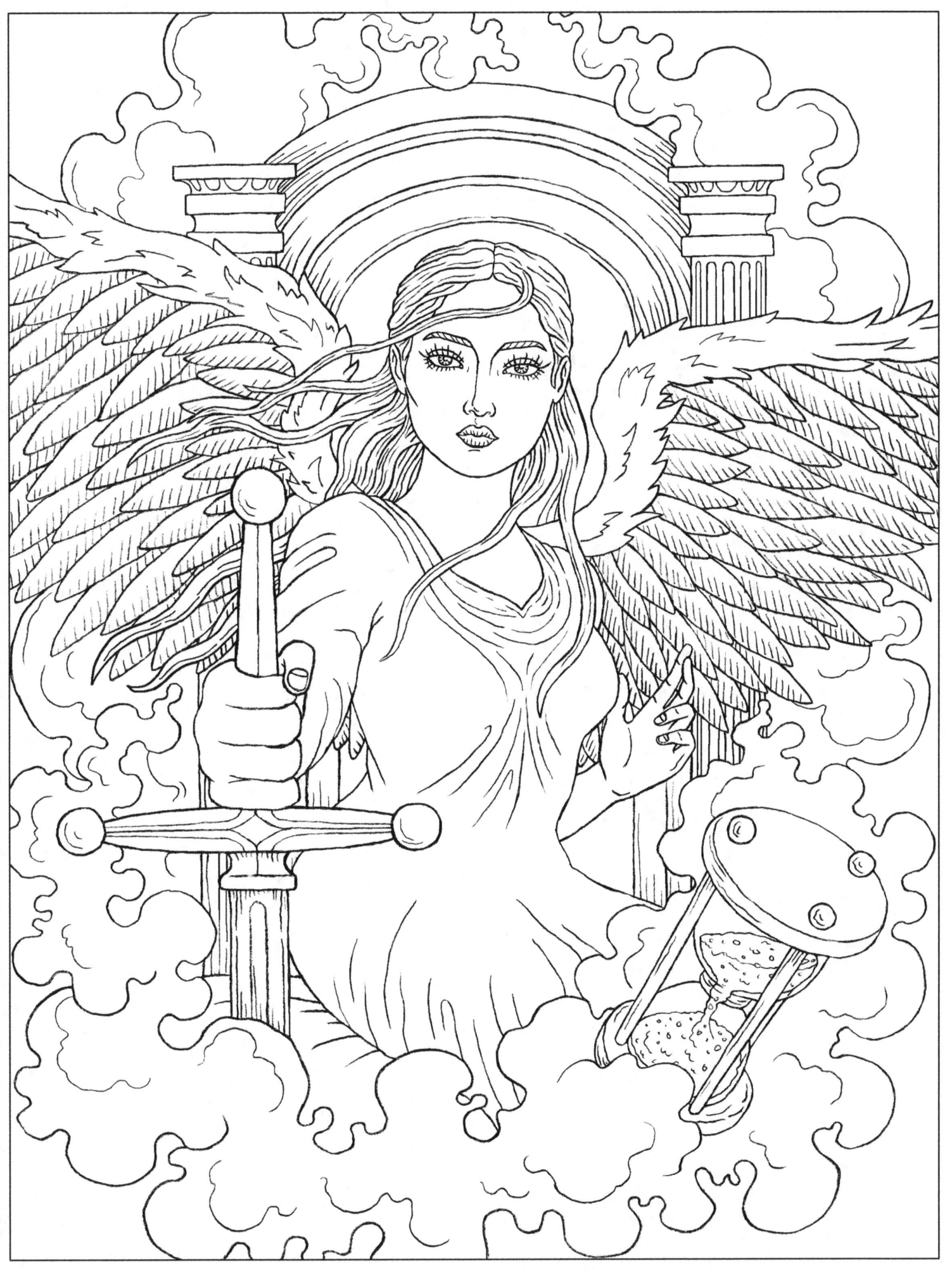

48

ALSO AVAILABLE FROM VIVID PUBLISHERS

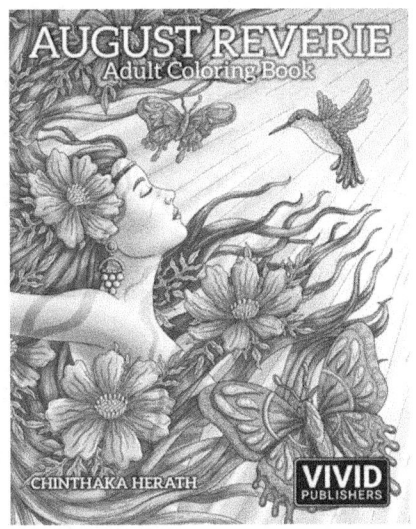

August Reverie

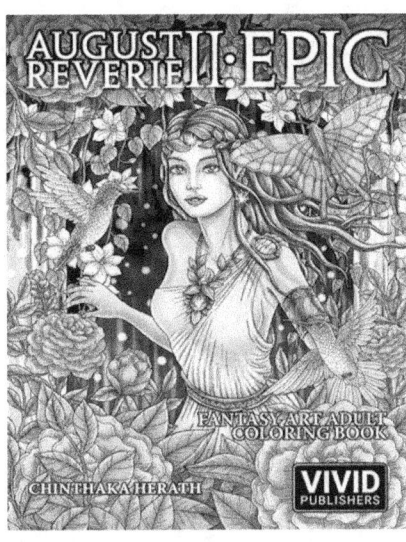

August Reverie 2: Epic

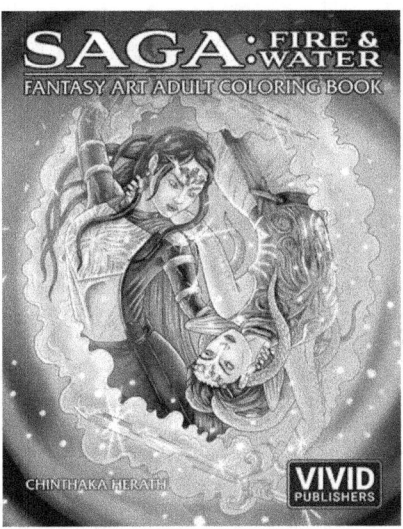

Saga: Fire & Water

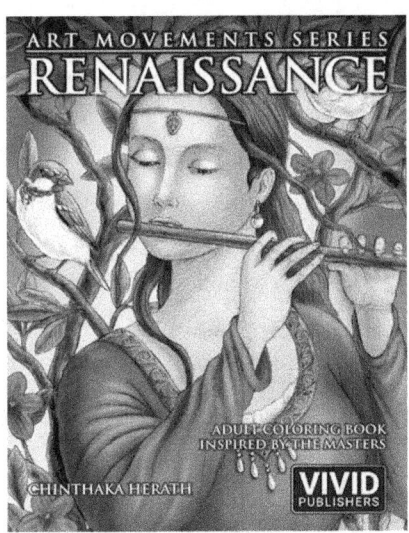

Art Movements Series: Renaissance

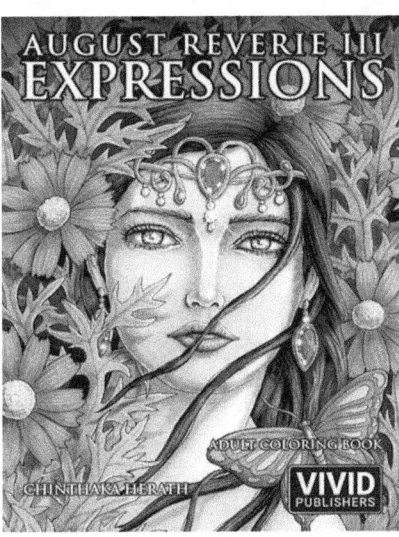

August Reverie 3: Expressions

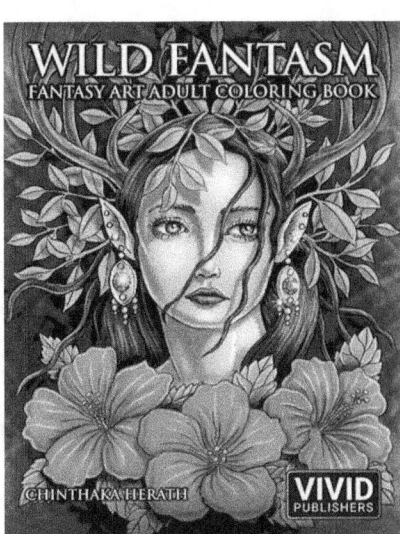

Wild Fantasm

Preview all the pages at www.vividpublishers.com/books

www.ingramcontent.com/pod-product-compliance
Lightning Source LLC
Chambersburg PA
CBHW080533220526
45465CB00006B/2695